INVENTIONS AND DISCOVERY

PHILO FARNSWORTH and the

TELEVISION

by Ellen Sturm Niz

illustrated by Keith Tucker

Consultant:

Raissa Allaire, Vice President/Chief of Staff
Museum of Broadcast Communications
Chicago, Illinois

Capstone
press®
Mankato, Minnesota

Graphic Library is published by Capstone Press,
151 Good Counsel Drive, P.O. Box 669, Mankato, Minnesota 56002.
www.capstonepress.com

1 2 3 4 5 6 11 10 09 08 07 06

Library of Congress Cataloging-in-Publication Data
Niz, Ellen Sturm.
 Philo Farnsworth and the television / by Ellen Sturm Niz; illustrated by Keith Tucker.
 p. cm.—(Graphic library. Inventions and discovery)
 Summary: "In graphic novel format, tells the story of how Philo Farnsworth came up with
the idea for electronic television at age 14, and later developed his idea into the technology for
television that is still used today"—Provided by publisher.
 Includes bibliographical references and index.
 ISBN-13: 978-0-7368-6487-9 (hardcover)
 ISBN-10: 0-7368-6487-3 (hardcover)
 ISBN-13: 978-0-7368-7522-6 (softcover pbk.)
 ISBN-10: 0-7368-7522-0 (softcover pbk.)
 1. Farnsworth, Philo Taylor, 1906–1971—Juvenile literature. 2. Electric engineers—United
States—Biography—Juvenile literature. 3. Inventors—United States—Biography—Juvenile
literature. 4. Television—History—Juvenile literature. I. Tucker, Keith, ill. II. Title. III. Series.
TK6635.F3N59 2007
621.3880092–dc22
[B]   2006006395

Art Direction and Design
Jason Knudson and Juliette Peters

Colorist
Tami Collins

Editor
Christine Peterson

Editor's note: Direct quotations from primary sources are indicated by a yellow background.

Direct quotations appear on the following pages:
Page 15, from an interview with Elma Farnsworth as published in *The Boy Who Invented Television: A Story of Inspiration, Persistence, and Quiet Passion* by Paul Schatzkin (Silver Spring, Md.: TeamCom Books, 2002).
Page 21, from David Sarnoff's speech at the 1939 World's Fair as published in *Looking Ahead: The Papers of David Sarnoff* by David Sarnoff (New York: McGraw-Hill, 1968).
Page 25, quote attributed to Philo Farnsworth as published in *Distant Vision: Romance and Discovery on an Invisible Frontier* by Elma G. Farnsworth (Salt Lake City: PemberlyKent, 1990).

TABLE OF CONTENTS

By the early 1900s, people wanted better ways to communicate.

15

Thousands of people attended the showcase. The event was so popular it lasted for three weeks. Philo had to find new things to show on television.

This is what I hoped television would do. Bring people and information together.

Look, I'm on television!

The moon is more exciting to see on television than in the sky.

In 1937, Philo formed the Farnsworth Television and Radio Corporation. By 1939, his company had made its first television sets.

Philo won the patent battle, but RCA had more money and power. In April 1939, Sarnoff introduced television at the New York World's Fair.

And now we add radio sight to sound.

I give you television! This new technology is sure to change society.

The event was broadcast on the fairgrounds and to a few televisions RCA had installed in New York.

Later that week, the first televisions went on sale in New York City.

Can we buy a television, Dad?

I'm afraid not. It would take six months of my pay to buy one of those.

$600

CHAPTER 4
TELEVISION NATION

Philo was out of the television business just as his invention took off. By 1950, at least 6 million television sets were in American homes. By the next year, television networks were broadcasting from coast to coast.

In 1951, the first color television program was broadcast. Regular color television broadcasts began in 1953.

We're nearly sold out of color televisions. You may want to buy one now.

$1,000.

Color TV

SALE

Color televisions are too expensive. We'd like a black-and-white television instead.

Philo's invention has continued to grow. Today, most U.S. homes have two or more television sets.

Television changed how people spend their time.

Today, people rely on television for news and entertainment.

MORE ABOUT FARNSWORTH AND THE TELEVISION

 Philo T. Farnsworth was born August 19, 1906, in Beaver City, Utah. He died March 11, 1971, at age 64.

 During World War II (1939–1945), Philo changed his Image Dissector into a sniperscope that made it possible for soldiers to see in the dark. He also developed a radar system that could spot and destroy an approaching missile for the military.

 In 1957, Philo was a guest on the television quiz show *I've Got a Secret*. No one on the panel could guess who he was. Host Gary Moore honored Philo by saying, "We'd all be out of work if it weren't for you."

 While Philo and his family lived in Fort Wayne, Indiana, they didn't have a television. When Philo's son Kent was in first grade, he discovered all his classmates had a television. Kent asked his dad to buy one for their family. Philo reluctantly agreed.

By 1967, almost every home had at least one television set. Today, most homes in the United States have at least two televisions. Most Americans watch more than four hours of television each day.

 Philo received at least 150 U.S. patents for his inventions.

 Time magazine named Philo one of the 100 most important people of the 20th century.

In 1994, Philo was named to the National Inventors Hall of Fame.

GLOSSARY

Image Dissector (IM-ij di-SEK-tur)—a machine that breaks images into electricity

Image Oscillite (IM-ij oss-UH-lyte)—a machine that receives an electronic signal and turns it into a television picture

invest (in-VEST)—to give or lend money to a company

license (LYE-suhnss)—a document that gives official permission to do something

network (NET-wurk)—a system of things that are connected to each other

patent (PAT-uhnt)—a legal document that gives an inventor the right to make, use, or sell an invention for a set number of years

INTERNET SITES

FactHound offers a safe, fun way to find Internet sites related to this book. All of the sites on FactHound have been researched by our staff.

Here's how:
1. Visit *www.facthound.com*
2. Choose your grade level.
3. Type in this book ID **0736864873** for age-appropriate sites. You may also browse subjects by clicking on letters, or by clicking on pictures and words.
4. Click on the **Fetch It** button.

FactHound will fetch the best sites for you!

READ MORE

Mattern, Joanne. *Television: Window to the World.* Reading Power. New York: PowerKids Press, 2003.

Nobleman, Marc Tyler. *The Television.* Great Inventions. Mankato, Minn.: Capstone Press, 2005.

Roberts, Russell. *Philo T. Farnsworth: The Life of Television's Forgotten Inventor.* Unlocking the Secrets of Science. Bear, Del.: Mitchell Lane, 2004.

Teitelbaum, Michael. *Radio and Television.* Great Inventions. Milwaukee: World Almanac Library, 2005.

BIBLIOGRAPHY

Everson, George. *The Story of Television; The Life of Philo T. Farnsworth.* New York: Arno Press, 1974.

Farnsworth, Elma G. *Distant Vision: Romance and Discovery on an Invisible Frontier.* Salt Lake City: PemberlyKent, 1990.

Schatzkin, Paul. *The Boy Who Invented Television: A Story of Inspiration, Persistence, and Quiet Passion.* Silver Spring, Md.: TeamCom Books, 2002.